GW01260709

SOME LATE LARK SINGING

RANDLE MANWARING

Randle Manwaring (signature)

Some late lark singing.......
The sundown splendid and serene

W.E. Henley

Brentham Press

First published 1992 by Brentham Press
40 Oswald Road, St Albans, Herts AL1 3AQ

ISBN 0 905772 34 2

A catalogue record for this book is available from
the British Library.

Printed in England by Mapro Publishing Services,
St Ives, Huntingdon, Cambs PE17 4AR

CONTENTS

KALEIDOSCOPE

THINGS PAST

THE HUMAN COMEDY

MORE THAN A GAME

SONGS OF PRAISE

Acknowledgments

Some of these poems have appeared or will appear
in:- *Anvil, Chichester Magazine, The Countryman,
The Cricketer, Envoi Anthology, Foolscap, Iota,
Kent & Sussex Poetry Society Anthology, News of
Hymnody, Ore, Outposts, Pennine Platform, Poetry
Nottingham, Wake Up,Stir About* (Unwin Hyman),
Weyfarers.

KALEIDOSCOPE

SWITZERLAND

This is the most charming place I have ever lived in
— Mark Twain

Here, an old revenant, I come
to find again, among the lakes,
Weggis, unchanged in twenty years
or a hundred since Mark Twain was here.
Guardians of the peace remain,
      the music and the laughter,
gathered wealth of centuries
and a calm neutrality
      pervade mountains and men,
      a confederacy of peace
in Catholic/Protestant equality.

THE FIDDLER OF WEGGIS

He makes Weggis unique
among lakeside resorts
for there, through every season,
he plays with poise and gusto,
    throwing himself, with violin,
    into all melodies
    of the western world
    from Strauss to Lloyd Webber.
Urbane in the extreme,
he will dance in ecstasy
melting distant snows
above the summer snow-line.

As leader of the trio
he provides a marked charisma,
a Maurice Chevalier
panache for each performance,
    while unattached, middle-aged
    women provide warm
    and constant adulation,
    as he smiles his winning way
through every lakeside concert,
singing the German songs
sotto voce, double-bass, piano
in obedient obligato.

PARADE OF THE STEAMERS, LUZERN

Sailing like old swans, they take the centre
stage, in proud remembrance of the days
        when singly, they criss-crossed the lake.

Now, on the launching date of a re-made ship,
they come again, full steam, in line abreast,
        decked overall, to celebrate.

Another season starts as a pale May sun
dapples the calm where an armada of ships
        follows the festive fleet of five.

Helicopters buzz the whole convoy,
chatter with hungry gulls at funnel height,
        answering the hooting of the veterans.

A holiday crowd along the promenade,
where chestnut candelabra mark the spring,
        joins in celebration.

Ageless snows on regal Mount Pilatus
welcome the paddle steamers' whirring wings,
        whispering Edwardian elegance.

CATRIONA LEAVES FOR IRELAND

A year since she came from the West of Ireland,
part of her training in catering,
came to this lakeside hotel in Locarno,
to Italianate Switzerland's playground
and the rigours of daily waitressing,
with insights into hotel management.

She has learned some secrets she cannot reveal,
unlearned a little of text-book dogma,
will match-up her judgment to further teaching,
be wiser than those who stayed at home,
comparing her wisdom with those in charge,
while adjusting her sights to a future career.

Italian waiters will press her no longer,
relieving of endless compliments;
they respected her power to hold her own
in a bustling world of male domination,
for the girl from Galway flies to Shannon,
changing trains at Bellinzona.

HANG-GLIDING ON THE SOUTH DOWNS

Against a background
of sky and earth,
the modern pterodactyl
wheels and floats,
a poem of movement,
winged strength
and stressed fragility.

Unearthly beauty
hangs at the mercy
of storm and currents,
the pilot sprawling
until he packs
his tricks in a long
dark trailer.

NARROW BOATS

Competing with cabin cruisers,
narrow boats invade the basin,
edging their way to the lock.

Water foams and like a toy
Curlew of Alveston and
Grace Darling wobble, locked in.

Out in the river they are again
mistress of their fate, down canals
and under bridges, seeming to own

waterways for which were built
such sturdy craft. Pleasure boats
look dismal by comparison.

SCHUMANN'S DEVOTION

In the first year of their brief marriage
he wrote this rhapsody for Clara,
she twenty-one; he thirty,
a few years before his darkness fell.

Young and adorable, he set her in
his. *Devotion* and, while she interpreted
into old age, his many works,
of this she was the interpreter.

STRATFORD GRAVES

In birthplace and parish church
his bones await the resurrection.
Anne's too, beside him, tell of seven
years she stayed beyond his time.

Outside, beneath the limes, are those
buried under paving stones
whose beauty and whose fame are lost –
Lucy and *Rose* is all we know.

A THEME OF PAGANINI

Virtuoso violinist,
send the message clear and strong
        to the girl you love.
Nor could a college band
or cultured orchestra
achieve such end result.

Paganini pizzicato
Paganini play, then see
        her come as come she will.
Not all the whimpering
of pop with microphones
can breathe the winning word.

Rapturised Rachmaninov
took up the selfsame theme, a song
        of timeless language,
reverberating still;
melodic masterpiece
spanning a century.

COLLECTED LETTERS

Autobiographers, please don't tell me the tale of your love life:
Much as it mattered to you, nothing could marvel me less.
- W.H. Auden

They say he wrote, on average, four a day
and died at ninety-four. A good output.
As Auden said - letters of thanks, letters from banks
but who kept what and why for publication
        years after the great man died?

How very dull or trivial most would seem,
those thousands of letters to small and great,
typed in haste or in spidery handwriting;
who wouldn't have thrown them all away,
        any time before he died?

Who cares what Felix wrote to Poppy darling
or if she sometimes called him Piggy? -
endearments spawned in predictable affairs,
so boring to all, except the contestants,
        in the years after they died.

Collected Poems - well, that's a different matter -
unseen gems, once mined and semi-polished,
unscrutinised by editorial eyes
but showing a clear development of style,
        unnoticed before he died.

Let Shaw or Churchill, Betjeman or Byron
be silent except through eloquent works.
If they had wished their intimacies made public
they could have arranged a tidy flow
        of royalties, before they died.

AFTER THE VISIT
(*Hardyesque*)

Unconsciously seeking
but never finding –
          a waiting game,
          played blindfold –
hoping against no hope,
he found, from time to time,
unexpected treasure.

BIG BANG

The Big Bang was long ago,
created in time
but still we feel
the pulse in everything
beating in the design where
great and small, life and death
flow in the poetry
of a universe.

THINGS PAST

TOOTING BEC, LONDON SW17

I

Where mammoth, wolf and wild deer roamed,
hunted by stone-age man through woodland swamps,
there came, in time, the culture of the Priory.

When Tooting was Tootinge, St Mary de Bec
managed the lands in feudal style
as part of the manor of Normandy.

II

Victorians heard the watercress man
calling *cress for your teas, if you please*,
as London overspill became the suburbs.

In twenty-six they built Bec School. A year
later, Jack Squire gave the prizes. At the flicks
Adolphe Menjou was in *Blonde or Brunette.*

III

In the thirties they made new roads – Gateside
and Lingwell, cradling the Malcolm MacArthurs,
the Douglas Aitkens and the Dennis Barnes,

children of Somme heroes and schooled at Bec,
tidy in blazers, blue and white caps,
grown into manhood before Dunkirk.

IV

Houses of strength and respectability
flourished around the rebuilt school,
in the seventies named after Ernie Bevin.

Who are they now, the lords of Tooting Bec?
Bevin died in fifty-one, Squire in fifty-eight
and plush seats for Menjou are a bingo hall.

V

Are Malcolm, Douglas and Dennis alive,
boys in *The Waste Land* then, where Eliot found
the gravel court and his thousand lost golf-balls?

Cultures have come and gone from Tooting,
scattered on the winds of the thousand years.
Quo vadis? asks the Filofaxed man on the Priory gate.

1930s RECESSION

With three million unemployed,
decay and disintegration rife
in dark, dank barns with rusty roofs,
farmsteads with their rotting walls,
crumbling thatch and slipping slates,
woodwork always left unpainted
        on tumbledown farms.

At weekends hikers came by train
and collectors of beetles, butterflies,
birds' eggs but arable tumbled
to grass. Loyal farm workers,
glad of a job, were no better off
than those who slaved in sweat shops
        in London's East End.

OFFICERS' RESETTLEMENT COURSE

Their final parade almost here,
they come for pre-natal exercises,
re-birth as civilians drawing near –
      Flight Lieutenants and Squadron Leaders,
      Wing Commanders and a few Group Captains
but for Air Vice-Marshals and the like
there are very special facilities.

They learn the secrets of applying for jobs,
CVs, body-language and interviews,
good health, sex, eating and drinking,
      financial know-how, taxation, insurance
      and how to relate to a lower income.
They will become sadder and wiser
as they invade a hard-nosed world.

In the club cloak-room this winter's day
are hung the fifty or sixty anoraks,
old duffle coats and donkey jackets,
      like a distant crowd of football faces,
      levelled in depersonalisation
these men are shedding a uniform glory
for a tawdriness few will ever shake off.

OLD AIRFIELDS

Back to the agricultural,
you will not know them now,
hedges dissuading runways
from optimistic take-off.
A Czech or Polish squadron
in years after Dunkirk
flew Hurricanes and Spitfires
where now only relics remain.

Farmhouse as officers' mess,
a barn OK for the sergeants,
all Nissen huts dismantled
but the shade of fighter pilots
may be felt on quiet evenings
and an engine thrust heard over
fields where poppies fringe
corn of the post-war summer.

KATYN

1940

Prime of Polish manhood
shot in murderous whim,
the incriminating date
fixing Stalin's crime.

1943

Charge and counter-charge,
the murder unconfessed,
uncovering the massive grave,
silent in Katyn forest.

1990

Kremlin yields at last
the truth of the massacre
of irreplaceable men,
leaders of their country.

CHURCH OF THE RECONCILIATION, EAST BERLIN
(Demolished, February 1985)

For over a hundred years, in Gothic splendour,
a church stood here, for reconciliation
but, with the building of the Berlin Wall,
was left unused by a divided nation.

Then, to provide a better field of fire
for Russian border guards sniping at trouble
it was destroyed, yet the surmounting cross,
blown skywards, managed to avoid the rubble.

ZION CHAPEL, NEWICK
(1834-1988)

As slavery ceased in the Colonies,
they opened the doors of the Chapel,
horse and trap bringing worshippers
from farm and trade, knowing their place
        in a settled religious order.

Traps were left by the road, horses
grazed in peace in the field behind
where now, in grave solemnity lie
rank upon rank, Westgates and Bennetts,
        leaving no descendants.

A tuning fork the only music
to start the singing until, one day,
a groaning harmonium, smuggled in,
gave some tunes to the little flock,
        wondering, as the world went by.

Through the long Victorian summer,
Edwardian autumn and wintry sixties,
the Chapel served a quiet dissent
until its slow and lingering death
        ended living epistles.

NOSTALGIA

She was always speaking of those days –
clothes rationing, utility furniture
and a pint of milk for a penny halfpenny.

No washing machines, fridges or freezers –
literally living from hand to mouth;
no *best buy, sell by*, pesticides, check-outs.

Blitz and bombing and home-grown food,
making do for weddings and baby things –
what a struggle it was in the hard old days.

He grew rather tired of the prices she quoted
and once hit back – *that was a day
when you could be run over by a horse and cart.*

THE HUMAN COMEDY

PRE-LUNCH DRINKS

None knowing all, we gathered
       in the ante-room,
introducing each other
       and our honoured guest.

Glancing in curiosity,
       we took in new faces,
impressed or unimpressed
       by first impressions.

Right on time, you came,
       the last arrival,
a burst of green and gold,
       dark-eyed and calm.

From that moment, the air
       was charged with a new
fair weather disturbance
       and a settled high pressure.

"SHE MARRIED THE MOST DISGUSTING MAN"
(Overheard in a Restaurant)

No envy escaped the informant's lips
as she made her observation:
this was the blatant, honest truth
of another woman's fate.

Was he uncouth in *all* his ways,
slopping food at every meal,
with munching sounds slushy and loud,
the manners of a pig?

Perhaps he never wiped his feet,
left toothpaste around the basin,
with clothes across the bedroom floor
in careless, reckless abandon.

Or did he never take a bath,
keeping his dirt in finger nails,
seldom changing his underpants –
this *most* disgusting man?

Whoever she fell in love with once
was now submerged beneath the filth,
but for better, for worse, in sweat and in grime
she *loves* her disgusting man.

THE CONSTANT WHISTLER

Whistling, to keep his spirits up,
to demonstrate his own bonhomie
tunes are pitched in the *tremulant*
voix celeste or *diapason*.

Snatches of hymns and rag-time merge,
switches of all-time favourites
float around the domestic scene,
piercing the stale, out-dated air.

He never sings; perhaps he cannot
and whistling is his compensation,
a way of saying something to us
we are not meant to understand.

MAD - AND HAPPY

Always a wave and a smile
for passing motorists,
      she takes her walks,
      all weathers, all seasons
and embodies
carefree contentment,
      owning little,
      knowing less.
Remember to return her joyous signals.

IN THE PSYCHIATRIC WARD

Thin walls divide
the living from the living –
no tell-tale uniform
of brisk officiousness.

Thin walls divide
the loving from the loved;
a quiet mind
in one but not the other.

Thin walls divide
psychosomatic
from the normal
heart-breaks of life.

Thin walls divide
the psychopath
from the psychiatrist's
near normality.

SMOKING

From rising bell to slow lights out
suffocating fumes crawl round
fleshy dungeons of the lungs
      taking in each other's smoke.

In every room residual whiffs
swirl and cling, settling down
in curtains, chairs, everywhere
      taking in each other's smoke.

Marking the future fight for breath,
ash falls in grey fragility
making no choice between man and wife
      taking in each other's smoke.

THE OLD BACHELOR

After years of home-grown splendour
and imagined independence,
a worsening decade brings decay,
an icy grip restricting movement.

The barricades went up fifty
years ago and there remain,
part of a small surrounded city
where relief is now impossible.

He might have made a huge mistake
or else have framed a new dimension,
passed on the life to him passed down,
but left the lineage incomplete.

Keep out, stay out, I own myself,
no one will share with me my pain
and wealth of individuality.
Let them have the inheritance tax.

SIGHT TESTING

In a windowless room of cavernous quiet
lights go on and off for reading
the bottom line,
while lenses click on the skeleton frame,
narrowed eyes might cheat to deny
their ageing sight.

Bicycle spokes must look clean to prove
a point, while red and green colour
the questioning.
Black circles darken or slightly fade,
then a text or two for reading off
at arm's length.

The prescription will soon be written out
with never an optical illusion
alluded to
but wait for squirting in the eyes
producing a number of soundless blinks
denying glaucoma.

WAITING

She waited for you through your nine months
of nonentity,
he also watching and waiting; the doctor
from a distance.

The rest of your life you waited – for *her*,
children, promotion,
letters, success, a new something;
now for retirement,

good wishes, the clock, more golf and bridge,
TV and then
you will wait for that unmentionable EXIT,
your waiting done.

AGEING

Who drew the tell-tale lines and when
engraved each fatal story,
then silently at a secret hour
robbed of a lifetime's glory?
impish hands, never caught in the act,
settled death's irreversible fact.

MORE THAN A GAME

DO NOT PICNIC ON THE CROQUET LAWN
(Notice in the gardens of Glyndebourne)

Rabbits have burrowed on the croquet lawn
and rusty hoops lie flat in heaps,
one end still marked by the coloured peg
but do not picnic, the notice says.

Lilies flower in their watery world,
earthed yet floating Ophelia like,
while over the hedges the sites are filled
and corks are popping in unison.

Do not panic on the croquet lawn
if you should decide to picnic there
for mallets have fallen to silence now,
holes only serving for putting practice.

BOUNDARY BOARDS
(Any County Cricket Ground)

Each match proceeds with grace
and pace; batsmen scamper,
fielders slide, bowlers stride
or trot; the contest ebbs and flows
to a conclusion:
Not so with boundary boards –
      Foster v. *Castlemaine*
      Woolwich v. *Halifax*
      Refuge v. *Britannic*
      Vauxhall v. *Toyota*
  local *Times* v. *Guardian* –
all contests undecided.

M.C.C.

Ernest Arthur, you should be with us now,
witnessing the climax of his cricket career,
for you put Colin on his winning way,
choosing those foretelling initials and
sending him to Homefield Prep. where Wally
coached. You were abroad but knew your son
was set for five years in the Tonbridge team,
then captaincy of Oxford, Kent and England.

Well done Ernest, your prognostications
right. Maybe you wrote, initially,
the full scenario of (Michael) Colin Cowdrey.

THE CLUB MAN

Every club needs one but only one.
He is the answer to every whim;
helps at the bar, stacks the chairs,
shouts to a player, *steady Jack*
and calls his fellow members *lads*.

He moves around at quite a pace
and even in the hottest weather
sports the cub tie; the embodiment
of social life, chain-smoking and
beer-bellied, clubbable, alone.

CHILDREN OF THE REGIMENT

A few years ago, as girls, they watched
furtively, half-interested, reading a book
then, with marriage to a county hero,
each settled for being a cricketing wife.

Now, with their babies, they continue watching
at home matches, engrossed in the welfare
of the little ones but when their men come home
from away fixtures just deal with dirty washing.

Once, their grandmothers, sent back to England
for their education, were children of another regiment,
the males serving at Simla or Snooty Ooty
and playing polo for the Bengal Lancers.

Wives of the county team, they enjoy a fame
for a few swift summers while husbands keep
a place in the premier side, with children
of once competing women and competitive males.

PRIMARY SCHOOL ARRIVING

A fluttering of dove-like hands –
I watch them waving by the wall
to children in the bare playground
      before the schoolday starts.

Why do they say these long good-byes,
reluctantly leaving the little ones,
when from their initial motherly tears
      have sprung delights of freedom?

Soon they will all outgrow the need
for the phantom umbilical cord,
resenting any show of affection
      which others might observe.

Many farewells will later occur
for longer, for good, for ill, who knows –
off for a trip around the world
      or another final wave?

SIXTH-FORM COLLEGE ARRIVING BY TRAIN

Make way for the refugee column
retreating from conventional schools,
by dress, behaviour and speech
all part of a pattern for living,
while T-shirt, trainers and jeans
lasted a generation,
now supported by long-sleeve woollies
and carrier-bags for files.

In the twenties, the lads were parading
in Oxford bags, blazers and pipes;
then, in the fifties, the winkle
pickers, long hair and Elvis
took over the fashionable stance.
Since then chippings from Sloane
Rangers, minis and bovver boots
take kaleidoscopic place.

A stream of learners is moving
resistlessly to make
a diversity of earners
and producers of goods for the world.
You see them, new-minted as always
presented with down-beat panache,
new styles emerging for ever
in timeless conformity.

NORTHEASE MANOR SCHOOL
(1963-1988)

Who would not, in body, mind and spirit
by years at Northease greatly benefit;
from boyhood through to youth, learning to be
a man coming to his maturity?

Looking across to Caburn, cowslip crowned
and down the valley where church towers are round,
he noticed Lewes Castle keping guard,
in summer sunlit and in winter starred.

He knew the brooks and meadows of the Ouse
and for his walks sometimes would idly choose,
by way of Rodmell and Piddinghoe,
to bring the town of Newhaven to view.

And so, with Northease years of gentle care,
fully himself, he soon became aware
that games on the ampitheatred playing field
and opened books, the fuller life revealed.

SONGS OF PRAISE

JOY TO ALL PEOPLE BRING
(For a Multi-Faith School Assembly)

Teach us all this morning, remind us all at night-time
We need each other's friendship as we're meeting
                                                face to face;
(Chorus)   So let the children sing,
            Joy to all people bring,
Trying hard to make the world a much happier place.

Give us more pleasure in our family and home-life
And not to think that being poor is any disgrace;
(Chorus)

May we show respect for what others will be feeling,
To realise we all need a small private space;
(Chorus)

Bind us all together with those from every country,
To take on board the differences of colour
                                                creed and race;
(Chorus)

(Commissioned by the publishers of *Wake up, Stir about*
specially for the English folk tune *Early One Morning*)

DECEMBER 25

His coming brought to an end the superstitions
left by the long ice-age when men wondered
    if the sun would expire in its grip.

In that universal winter the ungainly mammoth
had roamed the fields, the musk-ox and woolly
    rhinoceros grazing in Piccadilly.

So they chose, three hundred years after He died,
the heathen mid-winter festival of yule-logs
    and fir trees to celebrate the Birth.

CROPS

Drink your million million cups
of coffee or of tea
but think of those who grew the crops
in the old servility,
meeting the white man's greed for
profitability.

Meanwhile, the soil of Africa,
in despairing mood,
cries out for other harvests
for her people's good,
hoping the debt's repayment
will plant more vital food.

BISHOP OF DURHAM'S VISIT TO ST MICHAEL'S, CORNHILL, LONDON *(13 January 1987)*

Who will help to balance the Bishop
      with a touch of orthodoxy
and leaven the Durham message
      for Establishment in the City?
Oxford men will balance
      a rebel Oxonian don –
Peter Brooke of St Paul's Cathedral
      will surely frown upon
A Dunelm disturber of pigeons,
      tweaker of Anglican tails,
who must watch Ps and Qs in the City
      where conservatism always prevails.

BEFORE YOU GO

How can they maim the body of Christ,
      tearing it limb from limb,
weakening where already weak
      some vital part of Him?

Did they not hold the catholic faith,
      dividing on some minutiae,
leaving an impoverished, struggling flock
      in a state of penury?

Had they but stayed and worked away
      with patience and hope, they might
have altered beyond all recognition
      small churches in their plight.

Why did they leave the already too many
      churches along the way,
founding another structured sect,
      itself to be weakened one day?

BATHING AND WASHING

Accepting your free gift once and for all
we bathed to take away our human stain,
but now from daily work we come to you
our tired and dusty feet to wash again.

Always we live beneath your sheltering blood,
as once they did on that Passover night,
yet constantly we need its cleansing power,
reviving spirits weakened in the fight.

You laid aside your outer garments then,
taking the apron of a Roman slave,
then went to give away your very life
that we redemption's priceless gift might have.

And as we see the measure of your love,
stooping to make your servantship complete,
we ask that we, forgetting rank and power,
in genuine care may wash each other's feet.

SONG FOR A CHRISTIAN FUNERAL

We shall see him in the morning
        when the mists of life have cleared,
with his arms outstretched to greet us
        from a journey we have feared.

Those who toiled all night and struggled
        till the earthly fight was won
will awaken to the music
        of his welcoming "Well done!"

We shall recognise the Master
        with his wounded hands and side
as we worship him, the glorious,
        the ascended Crucified.

Though the shore now seems so distant
        we await the morning light
and the breakfast celebration
        when our faith gives way to sight.

A BIRTHDAY CARD

Thinking and reading, and scribbling,
poetry has been a way of life;
in people and places everywhere
there has often been a poem.

Sometimes a whisper in my ear
turns a pumpkin into a coach,
whilst from the treasury of living
much loveliness arises.

I believe in belief, I believe in love,
strong in the texture of creation,
despite the many tragedies
none can fully explain.

I have loved life and seen good days,
therefore I give the fullest praise
to my Creator, Sustainer, Redeemer,
weaving my eighty years.

also by Randle Manwaring

PROSE

THE HEART OF THIS PEOPLE (Quaintance, 1954)
A CHRISTIAN GUIDE TO DAILY WORK
     (Hodder, 1963)
THORNHILL GUIDE TO INSURANCE
     (Thornhill, 1976)
THE RUN OF THE DOWNS (Caldra House, 1984)
FROM CONTROVERSY TO CO-EXISTENCE
     (Cambridge University Press, 1985)
THE GOOD FIGHT (Howard Baker, 1990)
A STUDY OF HYMNWRITING AND HYMN-
SINGING IN THE CHRISTIAN CHURCH
     (Edwin Mellen Press, 1991)

POETRY

POSIES ONCE MINE (Fortune Press, 1951)
SATIRES AND SALVATION (Mitre Press, 1960)
UNDER THE MAGNOLIA TREE (Outposts, 1965)
SLAVE TO NO SECT (Mitre Press, 1966)
CROSSROADS OF THE YEAR* (White Lion, 1975)
FROM THE FOUR WINDS* (White Lion, 1976)
IN A TIME OF UNBELIEF (Henry Walter, 1977)
THANK YOU, LORD JESUS* (Henry Walter, 1980)
THE SWIFTS OF MAGGIORE (Fuller d'Arch Smith,
     1981)
IN A TIME OF CHANGE (Coventry Lanchester
     Polytechnic, 1983)
COLLECTED POEMS (Charles Skilton, 1986)

* For Children